Using the Standards
Data Analysis & Probability

Grade 4

Published by Instructional Fair
an imprint of
Frank Schaffer Publications®

Instructional Fair

Development House: MATHQueue, Inc.

Frank Schaffer Publications®

Instructional Fair is an imprint of Frank Schaffer Publications.

Printed in the United States of America. All rights reserved. Limited Reproduction Permission: Permission to duplicate these materials is limited to the person for whom they are purchased. Reproduction for an entire school or school district is unlawful and strictly prohibited. Frank Schaffer Publications is an imprint of School Specialty Publishing. Copyright © 2005 School Specialty Publishing.

Send all inquiries to:
Frank Schaffer Publications
8720 Orion Place
Columbus, Ohio 43240

Using the Standards: Data Analysis and Probability—Grade 4

ISBN: 0-7424-2994-6

3 4 5 6 7 8 9 10 QPD 10 09 08

Table of Contents

Introduction............4–5
Standards Correlation Chart..6
Pretest................7–8

Collection
Collecting Information........9
Ask Your Classmates.........10
Samples..................11
Match the Sample..........12
Bias.....................13
Facts Verses Opinions......14
Surveys in Everyday Life.....15
Create a Tally Chart........16
A Crossword Puzzle......17-18
Pictographs...............19
Line Plots................20
Bar Graphs.............21-22
Trend Graphs..........23-24
Line Graphs............25-26
Paper Route..............27
Make a Bar Graph.........28
Swimming Laps...........29
Let It Snow!..............30
Make a Trend Graph......31
Tell a Story..............32
Display Your Story.........33
Choose the Better Display....34
Which Type of Graph?......35
All Kinds of Graphs........36
Create Your Own Problems...37
Check Your Skills.......38-39

Analysis
The Mean................40
Means in the World........41
Middle of the Road........42
Find the Median..........43
Medians of the World......44
The Mode................45
Create a Data Set.........46

The Range................47
Home on the Range........48
Compare the Graphs.....49-50
A Helping Hand...........51
Cafeteria Duty............52
Way Out There...........53
One Big Bird..............54
Sketch the Plots...........55
Know the Terms..........56
Word Search.............57
Create Your Own Problems...58
Check Your Skills........59-60

Prediction
Basketball Practice......61-62
Snow Day.............63-64
Arts and Crafts.........65-66
Growth Rate...........67-68
The Dragonfly............69
Rattlesnakes...........70-71
A Puzzling Problem......72-73
True or False..........74-75
Let's Go to the Beach........76
Create Your Own Problems...77
Check Your Skills........78-79

Probability
Possible Verses Impossible....80
Things That Are Certain......81
Events in Your Life..........82
Likely and Unlikely Events....83
On a Roll................84
More Events..............85
Outcomes................86
Tree Diagrams..........87-88
Make a Tree Diagram......89
Predicting Outcomes.......90
Experiments..............91
Roll the Dice.............92
Conduct an Experiment......93

Is That Fair?..............94
Designing a Fair Game......95
Probability................96
The Probability Formula......97
Probability and Spinners.....98
Pick a Card...............99
A Decision-Making Spinner..100
Pizza Parlor..........101-102
Getting Dressed..........103
A Probability Riddle....104-105
Create Your Own Problems..106
Check Your Skills.....107–108

Post Test..........109-110
Answer Key........111-120
Vocabulary Cards....121-128

Introduction

This book is designed around the standards from the National Council of Teachers of Mathematics (NCTM), with a focus on data analysis and probability. Students will build new mathematical knowledge, solve problems in context, apply and adapt appropriate strategies, and reflect on processes.

The NCTM process standards are also incorporated throughout the activities. The correlation chart on page 6 identifies the pages on which each NCTM data analysis and probability substandard appears. Also look for the following process icons on each page.

 Problem Solving   Communication   Reasoning and Proof

 Connections   Representation

Workbook Pages: These activities can be done independently, in pairs, or in groups. The problems are designed to stimulate higher-level thinking skills and address a variety of learning styles.

Problems may be broken into parts, with class discussion following student work. At times solution methods or representations are suggested in the activities. Students may gravitate toward using these strategies, but they should also be encouraged to create and share their own strategies.

Many activities will lead into subjects that could be investigated or discussed further as a class. You may want to compare different solution methods or discuss how to select a valid solution method for a particular problem.

Communication: Most activities have a communication section. These questions may be used as journal prompts, writing activities, or discussion prompts. Each communication question is labeled **THINK** or **DO MORE**.

Introduction (cont.)

Create Your Own Problems: These pages prompt students to create problems like those they completed on the workbook pages. Encourage students to be creative and to use their everyday experiences. The students' responses will help you to assess their practical knowledge of the topic.

Check Your Skills: These activities provide a representative sample of the types of problems developed throughout each section. These can be used as additional practice or as assessment tools.

Vocabulary Cards: Use the vocabulary cards to familiarize students with mathematical language. The pages may be copied, cut, and pasted onto index cards. Paste the front and back on the same index card to make flash cards, or paste each side on separate cards to use in matching games or activities.

Assessment: Assessment is an integral part of the learning process and can include observations, conversations, interviews, interactive journals, writing prompts, and independent quizzes or tests. Classroom discussions help students learn the difference between poor, good, and excellent responses. Scoring guides can help analyze students' responses. The following is a possible list of problem-solving steps. Modify this list as necessary to fit specific problems.

1—Student understands the problem and knows what he or she is being asked to find.

2—Student selects an appropriate strategy or process to solve the problem.

3—Student is able to model the problem with appropriate manipulatives, graphs, tables, pictures, or computations.

4—Student is able to clearly explain or demonstrate his or her thinking and reasoning.

NCTM Standards Correlation Chart

		Problem Solving	Reasoning and Proof	Communication	Connections	Representation
Collection	consider how data collection affects a data set	12, 19, 20, 21	11, 12, 13,	9, 10, 16, 17,	10, 11, 14,	9, 14, 19, 20, 21,
	collect and organize data	22, 23, 24, 25,	32, 35	18, 27, 28, 29,	15, 16	22, 23, 24, 25
	represent data in tables and graphs	26, 34, 36		30, 31, 32, 33		26, 33, 34, 36
	represent categorical and numerical data					
Analysis	describe the shape of a data set	46, 49,	46, 53, 54	51, 52, 55,	40, 41, 42,	40, 42, 43, 45, 47, 48,
	use measures of center	50, 55		56, 57	44, 45, 48	49, 50, 51, 52, 53
	compare data representations					
Prediction	propose and justify predictions based on data and design and further investigate conclusions or predictions	61, 62, 70, 71	65, 66, 69, 72, 73, 74, 75, 76	63, 64, 67, 68, 72, 73, 76	61, 62, 69, 70, 71	63, 64, 65, 66, 67, 68, 74, 75
Probability	describe the degree of likelihood of events	89, 91, 99,	80, 81, 82, 83, 84,	82, 85, 86, 89, 92,	80, 83, 87, 88,	81, 84, 86, 87,
	predict probabilities of outcomes and test predictions	101, 102, 103	90, 93, 94, 96, 98, 100	93, 95, 101, 102, 104, 105	90, 91	88, 92, 96, 97, 98, 99, 100, 104, 105
	represent the likelihood of an event with a number from 0 to 1					

The pretest, post test, Create Your Own Problems, and Check Your Skills pages are not included on this chart, but contain a representative sampling of the process standards. Many pages also contain THINK or DO MORE sections, which encourage students to communicate about what they have learned.

Pretest

Use the bar graph to answer questions 1 – 4.

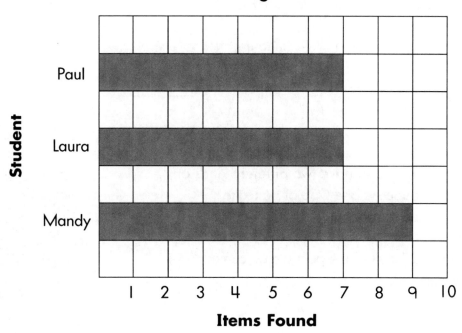

1. Which student found the most items in the scavenger hunt?

   _____

2. How many items did Paul find?

   _____

3. How many more items did Mandy find than Laura?

   _____

4. What is the mode number of scavenger hunt items found?

   _____

Pretest

5. Thomas scored 3, 1, 2, 1, and 3 goals in five games this season. Find the mean, median, mode, and range of the data.

mean: _____   median: _____

mode: _____   range: _____

A restaurant offers three different kinds of pancakes: buttermilk, whole wheat, and blueberry. They also have two different kinds of syrup: maple and lite maple. Suppose one type of pancake and one type of syrup is chosen at random.

6. Make a tree diagram to list all of the possible outcomes. How many possible outcomes are there?

_____

7. Which type of pancake is most likely to be picked? Explain.

_____

8. What is the probability of picking blueberry pancakes with lite maple syrup?

_____

Collection

Name _____ Date _____

Collecting Information

Asking questions in a **survey** is a way to gather information called **data**.

After you conduct a survey, you can organize the data in a **tally chart**.

Directions: Benjamin surveyed 17 fourth graders about their favorite type of pet.

Complete the tally chart.

Favorite Kind of Pet		
Pet	**Tally**	**Number**
Dog		8
Cat		3
Fish		4
Bird		2

THINK

What purpose does the Tally column serve in a tally chart?

Collection

Name _____ Date _____

Ask Your Classmates

Directions: Think of a survey question that you can ask your classmates. The question should have 3 to 5 possible answers. For example, you might ask them to name their favorite color or their favorite sport.

Organize the results in a tally chart.

THINK

Did anyone give an answer to your survey question that you did not expect? If so, how did you handle this situation?

Samples

The people that you survey typically represent a larger group because the group you want to study is too large to survey everyone.

The people you question are a **sample** of the larger group. It is important to find a sample that represents the larger group fairly.

For example, suppose you want to know the favorite weekend activity of 4th graders. If you conduct your survey at the beach on a weekend, many students will likely say they enjoy going to the beach. This sample will not be a good representation of all 4th graders.

Directions: Read each situation. Tell whether or not the sample being surveyed fairly represents the larger group. Circle yes or no.

1. Larger group: students who enjoy walking to school
   Sample: students getting off the bus in the morning

   yes   no

2. Larger group: people who like to garden in your city
   Sample: customers at a local gardening store on a Saturday afternoon

   yes   no

3. Larger group: fourth graders who like the zoo
   Sample: all 9-year olds at the zoo during a field trip

   yes   no

4. Larger group: all the students in your school that like recess
   Sample: 25 students on the playground during recess

   yes   no

Collection

Name _____ Date _____

Match the Sample

Directions: Amy is conducting a survey to learn about each group of people. Identify a sample of people to ask.

1. people who rent 2 or more movies each month

   _____

2. pet owners in your town

   _____

3. people who are shopping for a new car

   _____

4. grocery store shoppers in your town

   _____

5. people who like eating Chinese food

   _____

THINK

What will happen if you survey a sample of people that does not represent the larger group? Explain.

Collection

Bias

Bias occurs when a sample does not represent the larger group. An **unbiased** sample will give accurate results. However, a biased sample can lead to invalid conclusions.

Directions: Explain why the sample in each of the following surveys is biased. Give an example of a sample that would be unbiased.

1. Christina wants to know the favorite foreign language of students at her high school. She surveys 15 students from the Spanish club and 15 students from the German club.

2. Albert is conducting a survey about the favorite snack of fourth graders at his school. He surveys every other student who buys pretzels in the school cafeteria.

Name _____ Date _____

Facts Verses Opinions

The data collected in a survey can either be facts or opinions.

A **fact** is actual information, such as a what kind of car a person drives.

An **opinion** describes how a person feels about something, such as a favorite movie.

Directions: Tell whether each statement is a fact or an opinion. Circle the correct answer.

1. The outside temperature is 82°F right now.   fact   opinion

2. Popcorn is my favorite kind of snack.   fact   opinion

3. Molly is the best player on the team.   fact   opinion

4. Mr. Reynolds is a great school principal.   fact   opinion

5. Calvin is 54 inches tall.   fact   opinion

6. Ralph scored 3 goals in a soccer game.   fact   opinion

DO MORE

Give another example of a fact and another example of an opinion.

Collection   Name _____ Date _____

Surveys in Everyday Life

Directions: Find an example of a survey in a newspaper, in a magazine, online, or on television. Have an adult help you to understand the survey and answer each question. Use the survey and your answers below to complete page 16.

1. Where did you find the survey?

   _____

2. What question or questions are being asked by the survey?

   _____

3. What sample of people is being surveyed?

   _____

4. What larger group does the sample represent?

   _____

5. Does the survey present its data as facts or opinions?

   _____

Collection

Name _____ Date _____

Create a Tally Chart

Directions: Create a tally chart of the survey you found when you completed page 15.

THINK

Is there anything about charting surveys with real data that makes it difficult? Explain.

A Crossword Puzzle

Directions: Fill in each blank. Use your answers to complete the crossword puzzle on page 18. Each word will be used once.

| survey | sample | opinion |
| data | fact | bias | tally |

Across

2. Surveys are usually conducted using a _____ of a larger group.

3. If a sample does not represent the larger group, there may be _____ in the survey.

6. The results of a survey can be organized in a _____ chart.

7. _____ can be either facts or opinions.

Down

1. An _____ describes how someone feels about something.

4. A _____ is a way to collect information by asking questions.

5. The goal of a survey is to collect data, which may be a _____ or an opinion.

A Crossword Puzzle

Directions: Use your answers from page 17 to solve the crossword puzzle.

Name _____ Date _____

Pictographs

A **pictograph** is a way to display data using pictures.

The **key** of the pictograph tells what each picture represents.

Directions: Use the pictograph to answer each question.

Number of Books Read

Carlton	📕 📕 📕 📕
Suzie	📕 📕
Alfonso	📕 📕 📕 📕 📕
Penelope	📕 📕 📕 📕

Key: 📕 = 2 books

1. Which student read the most books? _____

2. How many books does each picture represent? _____

3. How many more books did Carlton read than Suzie? _____

THINK

How is reading 1 book represented in the pictograph?

Line Plots

A **line plot** displays data along a number line.

Directions: Each student in Mr. Himebaugh's science class worked on a science fair project. The line plot shows how many hours the students spent working on their projects. Use the line plot to answer each question.

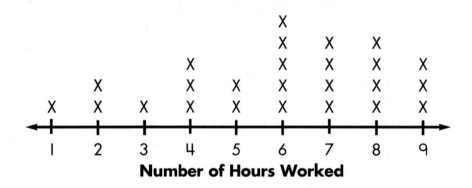

Number of Hours Worked

1. How many students are in Mr. Himebaugh's class? _____

2. How many students worked for exactly 8 hours? _____

3. How many students worked for at least 7 hours? _____

4. How many students worked no more than 4 hours? _____

DO MORE

What length of hours worked was most common in Mr. Himebaugh's class?

Collection Name _____ Date _____

Bar Graphs

Bar graphs use the height of bars to display and compare data.

Directions: Use the bar graph to answer the questions on page 22.

Mr. Davis' fourth grade class went on a field trip to a wilderness camp. Afterwards, each student was asked to name his or her favorite outdoor activity.

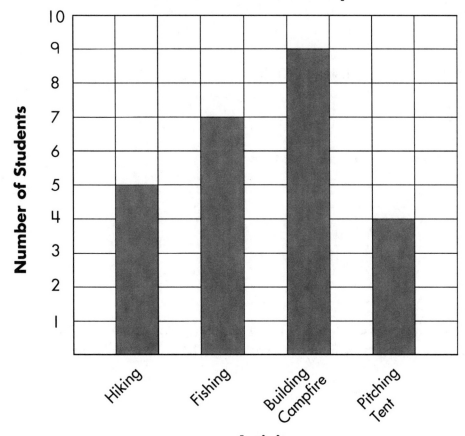

Bar Graphs

Directions: Use the bar graph on page 21 to answer each question.

1. How many students went on the field trip? _____

2. What was the most popular activity in Mr. Davis' class? _____

3. What was the least popular activity in Mr. Davis' class? _____

4. How many more students voted for fishing than for pitching a tent? _____

5. How many students voted for an activity other than building a campfire? _____

THINK

Miss Wallace's fifth grade class took 4 more students to the camp than Mr. Davis' fourth grade class. How many students are in Miss Wallace's class?

Collection

Name _____ Date _____

Trend Graphs

A **trend graph** uses a line above the bars of a bar graph to show the trend in data over time.

Directions: Use the trend graph to answer the questions on page 24.

A farmer plowed several fields this week.
The trend graph shows how many acres he plowed each day.

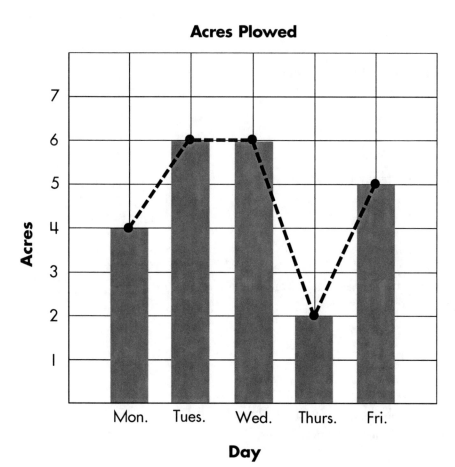

Collection

Trend Graphs

Directions: Use the trend graph on page 23 to answer each question.

1. On which days did the farmer plow the greatest number of acres? _____

2. On which day did he plow the fewest number of acres? _____

3. How many acres did the farmer plow altogether? _____

4. How many more acres did the farmer plow on Friday than Thursday? _____

5. Between which two days did the number of acres plowed stay the same? _____

THINK

Why might the number of acres plowed on Thursday have been so much lower than the other days?

Line Graphs

A **line graph** uses line segments to show how data changes over time.

Directions: Ramey made a line graph to show how a flower grew over time. Use the line graph to answer the questions on page 26.

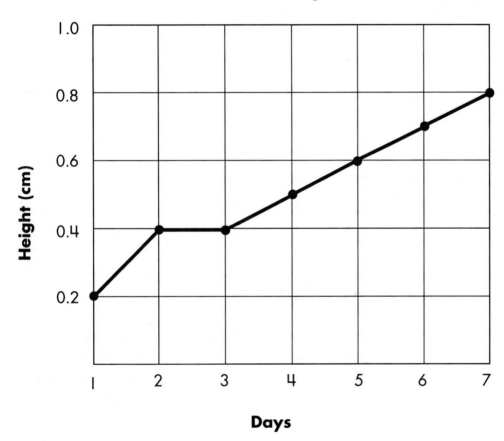

Line Graphs

Directions: Use the line graph on page 25 to answer each question.

1. What was the height of the flower on day 2?

   _____

2. What was the height of the flower on day 5?

   _____

3. Between which two days did the flower grow the least?

   _____

4. Between which two days did the flower grow the most?

   _____

5. How much did the flower grow in all?

   _____

Paper Route

Directions: Five friends have a paper route in their neighborhoods. The number of newspapers they each deliver is shown in the table. Make a pictograph of the data. Be sure to include a title for the graph and a key telling how many papers each picture represents.

Name	Newspapers
Mary	20
Thomas	50
Jasmine	60
Ricardo	40
Paul	30

Collection Name _____ Date _____

Make a Bar Graph

Directions: Make a bar graph using the data in the tally chart. Be sure to include a scale, the labels, and a title.

Favorite Type of Juice		
Type of Drink	**Tally**	**Number**
Apple Juice	𝍷𝍷𝍷𝍷𝍷 |||	8
Grape Juice	𝍷𝍷𝍷𝍷𝍷 ||	7
Orange Juice	𝍷𝍷𝍷𝍷𝍷		6
Cranberry Juice	||	2

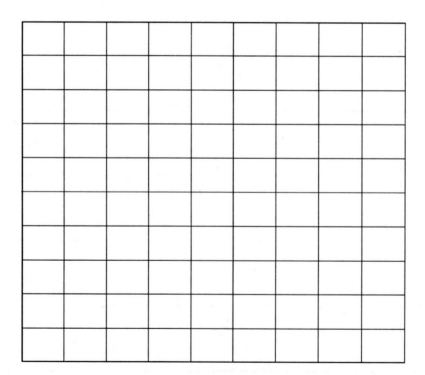

Collection Name _____ Date _____

Swimming Laps

Directions: The table shows how many laps students in a gym class swam today. Make a line plot of the data.

Laps	1	2	3	4	5	6	7	8
Number of Students	1	3	3	4	6	5	3	1

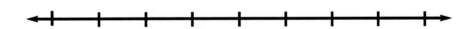

THINK

How did you decide which set of numbers to put on the number line and which set to make the Xs? Explain.

Collection

Let It Snow!

Directions: Oscar measured the amount of snow on the ground every 2 hours during a snow storm. Make a line graph of the data.

Time	Snow (inches)
9:00 A.M.	1
11:00 A.M.	3
1:00 P.M.	4
3:00 P.M.	5
5:00 P.M.	8

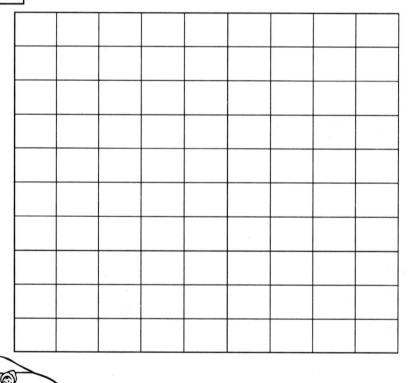

Collection

Make a Trend Graph

Directions: Make a trend graph using the data in the chart. Be sure to include a scale, the labels, and a title.

Hours	1	2	3	4	5	6	7	8
Rain (cm)	1	2	4	6	7	8	9	10

Name _____ Date _____

Tell a Story

Directions: Describe a situation with data that can be represented by each type of graph.

1. bar graph

2. line plot

3. line graph

4. pictograph

THINK

Could either of these situations be represented by a trend graph? Explain.

Display Your Story

Directions: Draw a graph for each situation that you wrote on page 32.

1. bar graph

2. line plot

3. line graph

4. pictograph

Choose the Better Display

Directions: George wants to display the results of a survey he conducted. Should he use the bar graph or the line graph? Discuss the answer with your classmates.

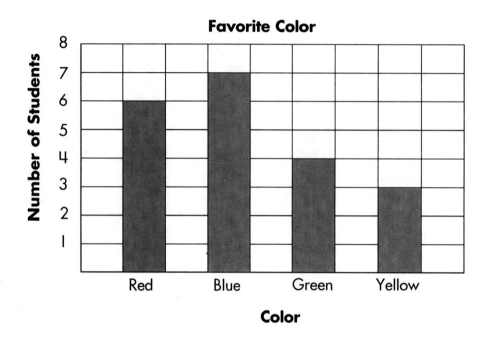

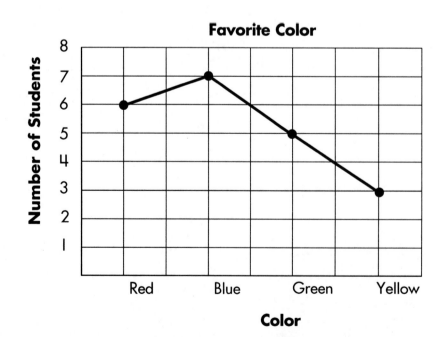

Which Type of Graph?

Directions: List an appropriate graph for each situation.

1. Terrance and his scout group went on a 4-day hike. On the first day they hiked 3 miles, on the second day they hiked 5 miles, on the third day they hiked 4 miles, and on the fourth day they hiked 8 miles.

   _____

2. Jamie's class took a math quiz worth 5 points. Three students earned 1 point, four students earned 2 points, four students earned 3 points, six students earned 4 points, and seven students earned 5 points.

   _____

3. Andy conducted a survey among his classmates to find their favorite type of car. Students could choose between sports cars, sedans, pickup trucks, SUVs, and minivans.

   _____

THINK

Can any of the situations above be modeled by more than one type of graph? Explain.

All Kinds of Graphs

Directions: Write the type of graph that is being described in each question.

1. I am very good at comparing information between different categories. I use bars of different lengths to represent data. What type of graph am I?

   _____

2. I can represent data that is collected over time. I use data points and line segments to display data. What type of graph am I?

   _____

3. I like to compare data that can be counted. I use pictures and symbols to represent data. What type of graph am I?

   _____

4. I can show how numerical data are grouped together by marking data points on a number line. What type of graph am I?

   _____

Create Your Own Problems

1. Write a word problem about the following line plot.

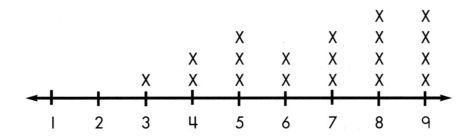

2. Write a question about choosing which type of graph to use for displaying data.

3. Write a story problem about choosing an unbiased sample for a survey.

4. Write a question about conducting a survey with an unbiased sample of a larger group.

Collection

Check Your Skills

1. Give an example of a biased sample of a larger group.

   _____

2. Give an example of a unbiased sample of a larger group.

   _____

3. Create a bar graph of the data shown in the table.

Puzzles Solved		
Student	**Tally**	**Number**
Christian	IIII	4
Vicky	III	3
Alfonso	̶I̶I̶I̶I̶ I	6

Collection Name _____ Date _____

Check Your Skills (cont.)

Use the line graph to answer questions 4 – 7.

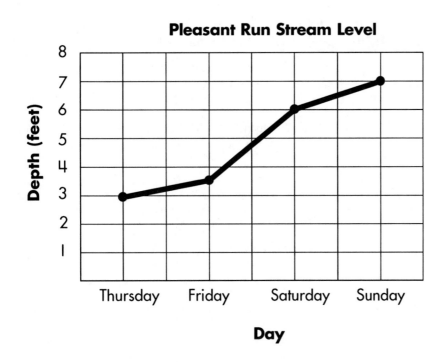

4. What was the depth of Pleasant Run stream on Friday? _____

5. How much did the depth of Pleasant Run stream increase between Thursday and Friday? _____

6. Between which two days did the depth of Pleasant Run stream increase the most? _____

7. Between which two days did the depth of Pleasant Run stream increase the least? _____

Analysis   Name _____ Date _____

The Mean

> The average of a data set is the **mean**.
>
> To find the mean of a set of data, add the values in the set of data. Then divide by the number of values in the data set.

Directions: Find the mean of each set of data. Show your work.

1. number of pennies:
   213, 644, 127

   _____

2. number of dollars raised:
   $32, $74, $89

   _____

3. number of magazines sold:
   234, 753, 362, 463

   _____

4. length of cars (in feet):
   6.8, 7.9, 8.3, 7.5. 8.5

   _____

THINK

How do think weather forecasters find the average daily temperature for a certain time of year? Explain.

Analysis Name _____ Date _____

Means in the World

Directions: Find the mean of each data set.

1.
Fastest Animals	
Animal	Speed
cheetah	70 mph
lion	50 mph
zebra	40 mph
rabbit	35 mph

_____

2.
Tallest Buildings	
Building	Height
Petronas Towers	1,483 feet
Sears Tower	1,450 feet
Jin Mao Building	1,381 feet

_____

3.
Highest Rollercoasters	
Rollercoaster	Height
Millennium Force	310 feet
Fujiyama	259 feet
Goliath	255 feet
Son of Beast	218 feet
Pepsi Max Big One	214 feet

_____

4.
Diameter of Planets	
Planet	Diameter
Mercury	3,032 miles
Venus	7,521 miles
Earth	7,926 miles
Mars	4,213 miles

_____

Analysis   Name _____   Date _____

Middle of the Road

When a group of data is ordered from least to greatest, the **median** is the middle number.

Directions: Find each median.

1.
Number of Cans Collected	
Third Graders	15
Fourth Graders	18
Fifth Graders	13

_____

2.
Number of Points Scored	
Peter	821
Nancy	657
Chad	714

_____

3.
Number of Miles Driven	
Eric	237
Suzanne	416
Alejandro	324
Gregory	552
Becky	319

_____

4.
Number of Dogs Walked	
Monday	6
Tuesday	8
Wednesday	5
Thursday	2
Friday	5

_____

THINK

How do you find the median if the numbers are ordered from greatest to least?

Analysis

Find the Median

Directions: Write each set of numbers in order from least to greatest. Circle the middle number to find the median.

1. 55, 21, 53, 28, 62

   _____

2. 432, 359, 752, 236, 537

   _____

3. 96, 33, 47, 58, 35, 23, 16

   _____

4. 263, 367, 469, 236, 258, 212, 674

   _____

5. 77, 43, 79, 182, 168, 155, 218

   _____

6. 22, 10, 16, 8, 11, 14, 25

   _____

THINK

Suppose a set of data has an even number of values. How do you think you would find the median? Explain.

Analysis   Name _____   Date _____

Medians of the World

Directions: Find the median of each set of data.

1. **Measure of Sound**

library	30 decibels
thunder	120 decibels
rocket engine	180 decibels
vacuum cleaner	70 decibels
hair dryer	80 decibels

   _____

2. **Animal Life Spans**

gorilla	20 years
rhinoceros	15 years
giraffe	10 years
horse	20 years
pig	10 years
polar bear	20 years

   _____

3. **Number of Building Stories**

Empire State Building	102 stories
Bank of China	70 stories
Shun Hing Square	81 stories

   _____

4. **Calories**

cheeseburger	300 calories
chocolate chip cookies	185 calories
vanilla ice cream	375 calories
raisins	40 calories
grape fruit	40 calories

   _____

The Mode

The **mode** is the number that occurs most often in a set of data.

Directions: Find the mode of each set of data.

1.

```
                    X
            X   X   X   X
            X   X   X   X
    X   X   X   X   X   X   X   X   X
    X   X   X   X   X   X   X   X   X
    ←———————————————————————————————→
    1   2   3   4   5   6   7   8   9
        Number of Fish Caught
```

_____

2.

Inches of Rain									
1	3	4	3	2	4	1	2	5
2	1	4	2	1	2	3	4	2

_____

THINK

Is it easier to find the mode from a table of data or from a line plot? Explain.

Analysis

Name _____ Date _____

Create a Data Set

Directions: Create a set of data with more than 4 elements for each of the following characteristics. It may help to display your data set in a line plot.

1. a mean of 4

2. a median of 3

3. a mode of 14

4. a median of 7, and a mode of 6

DO MORE

Create a data set that has the same mean, median, and mode.

Analysis   Name _____ Date _____

The Range

> The **range** is the difference between the greatest value and the least value in a data set.
>
> To find the range, subtract the smallest data value from the greatest data value.

Directions: Find the range of each set of numbers.

1. 13, 64, 25, 47, 79

   _____

2. 342, 645, 634, 538, 212

   _____

3. 65, 68, 29, 10, 153, 15

   _____

4. 234, 26, 357, 37, 669, 141, 138

   _____

5. 63, 43, 68, 89, 10, 81, 52

   _____

6. 120, 135, 467, 435, 147, 186, 239

   _____

THINK

Does the range tell you where the data are centered or how spread out they are? Explain.

Analysis   Name _____ Date _____

Home on the Range

Directions: Find the range of each data set.

1.
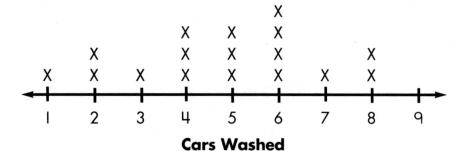
Cars Washed

_____

2.
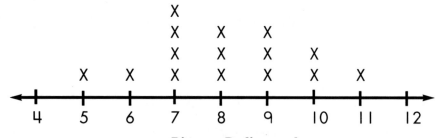
Pizzas Delivered

_____

3.
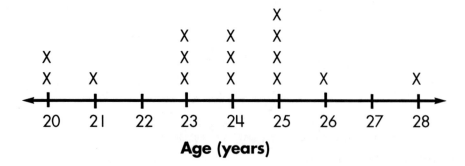
Age (years)

_____

Name _____ Date _____

Compare the Graphs

Directions: Use the two line plots to answer the questions on page 50.

Mr. Wilson and Miss Clark took their science classes into the woods to look for different kinds of leaves. The line plots show the number of students in each class who were able to find the number of leaves shown.

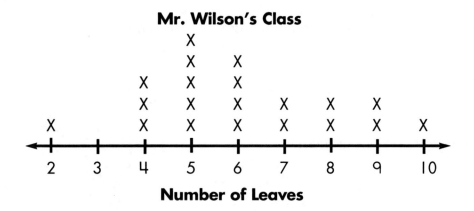

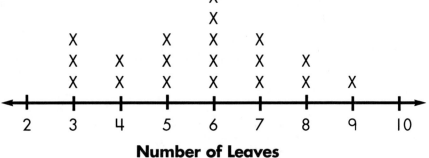

49

Name _____ Date _____

Compare the Graphs

Directions: Answer each question using the line plots on page 49.

1. In which class was the student who found the most leaves?

   _____

2. How many students in each class found 6 or more different kinds of leaves?

   _____

3. What is the range of each set of data?

   _____

4. What is the mode of each set of data?

   _____

5. Write a statement about each class that explains what the range tells you.

   _____

THINK

Which line plot has a greater range? Can you tell this just by looking at the graphs? Explain.

Analysis

A Helping Hand

Directions: Nick, Jill, and William volunteer their time helping out senior citizens in their neighborhood with chores. The bar graph shows how many hours they each spent volunteering last month. Find the mean, median, mode, and range of the data.

Volunteer Hours

Student: Nick, Jill, William

Number of Hours

mean: _____   mode: _____

median: _____   range: _____

Cafeteria Duty

Directions: Find the mean, mode, and range of the data in the pictograph.

Number of Sandwiches Made

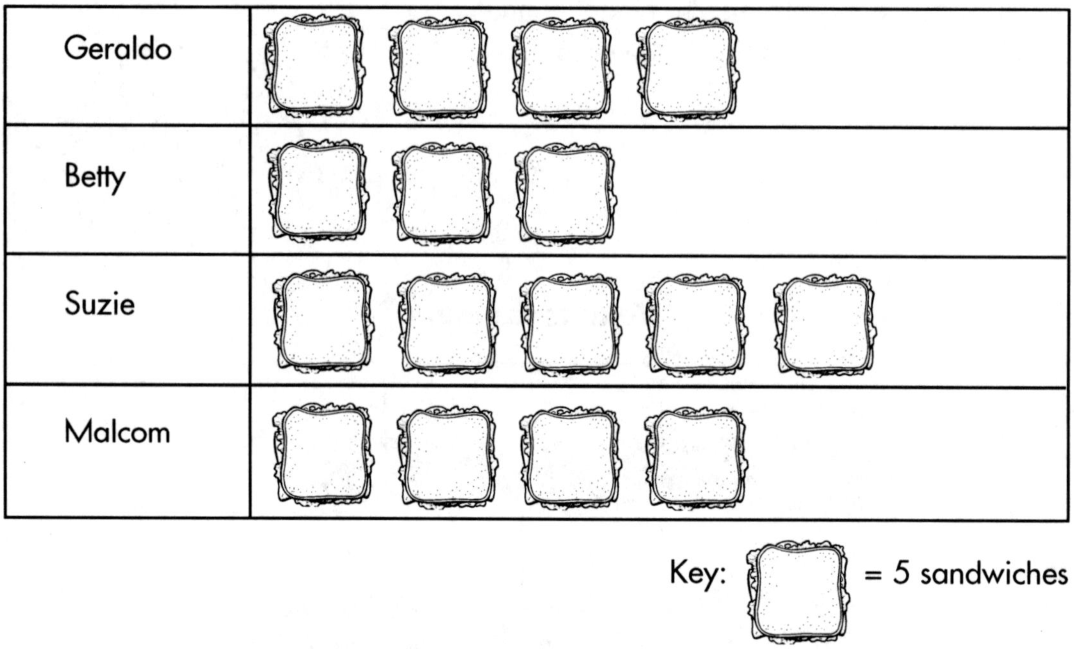

Geraldo	🥪 🥪 🥪 🥪
Betty	🥪 🥪 🥪
Suzie	🥪 🥪 🥪 🥪 🥪
Malcom	🥪 🥪 🥪 🥪

Key: 🥪 = 5 sandwiches

mean: _____

mode: _____

range: _____

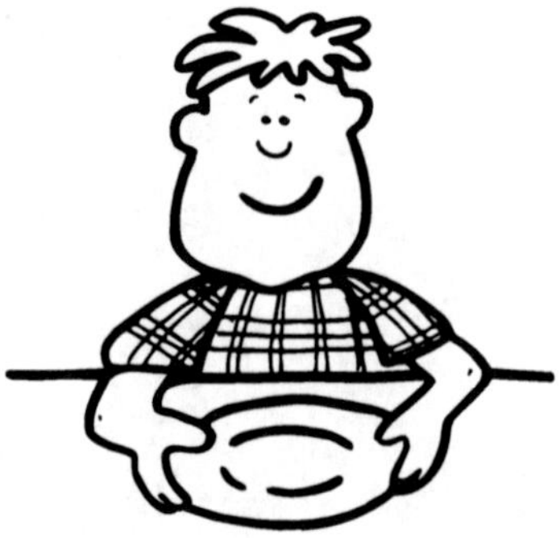

Analysis

Name _____ Date _____

Way Out There

Sometimes a set of data contains a value that is not typical of the other values in the set.

This type of data point is an **outlier**.

Directions: Identify the outlier in each set of data.

1.

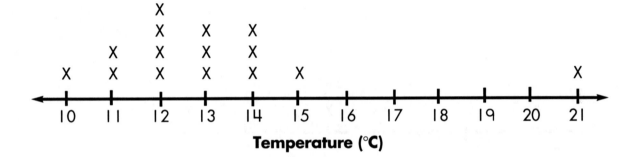

_____

2.

Age (years)									
22	41	21	56	33	41	63	38	36	
35	50	49	27	44	5	38	45	28	

_____

THINK

Do you think a data set can have more than one outlier? Explain.

Analysis

Name _____ Date _____

One Big Bird

Directions: Answer each question.

The largest bird in the world is the ostrich. Ostriches can grow up to 9 feet tall and weigh as much as 345 pounds. The line plot shows the heights of several ostriches.

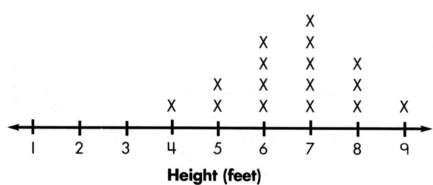

Height (feet)

1. How many ostriches are represented in the line plot?

   _____

2. What is the range in the heights of the ostriches?

   _____

3. Does there appear to be an outlier in the data? Explain.

   _____

Analysis

Name _____ Date _____

Sketch the Plots

Directions: Create two line plots with the following characteristics.

Two fourth grade classes took the same math test. The 1st period class had a higher range than the 3rd period class. The median grade was higher in the 3rd period class than the 1st period class.

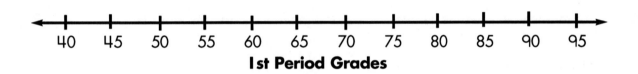
1st Period Grades

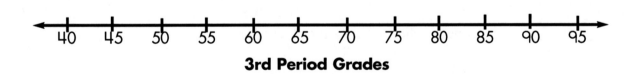
3rd Period Grades

DO MORE

Are there any outliers in either of your line plots? If not, add an outlier.

Analysis

Know the Terms

Directions: Fill in each blank. Then find your answers in the Word Search on page 57.

1. The value that occurs most often in a data set is the _____.

2. The _____ is the middle of a data set. Half the values are above it and half are below it.

3. The difference between the greatest value and the least value in a data set is the _____.

4. The _____ is the average.

5. A number that is not typical of the rest of a data set is an _____.

6. _____ is information that can be either fact or opinion.

Analysis

Name _____ Date _____

Word Search

Directions: Find each of your answers from page 56. Words may appear vertically or horizontally.

```
M C T F S P M I
O O U T L I E R
D A T A J L A A
E M E D I A N N
G A L O M W E G
A V E R A G E E
B N M A H D X S
```

DO MORE

What is another word for the mean?
Find it in the Word Search.

Analysis

Create Your Own Problems

1. Write a question about the median of a data set.

2. Write a question about finding the mode of a data set presented in a table.

3. Write a word problem that involves identifying outliers in a data set.

4. Write a question about the mean of a data set.

5. Write a question about using a line plot to find the range of a data set.

Check Your Skills

Use the line plot to answer questions 1 – 4.

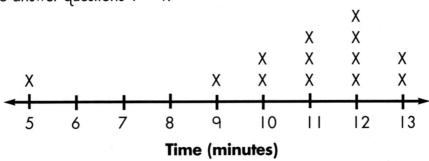

Time (minutes)

1. What is the median number of minutes?

   _____

2. What is the range in the number of minutes?

   _____

3. What is the mode of the data set?

   _____

4. Are there any outliers in the set of data? If so, identify them.

   _____

Check Your Skills (cont.)

5. George scored 8, 12, 11, and 9 points in 4 games. What is his mean number of points per game?

_____

6. The dogs at a veterinarian's office are 3, 6, 5, 4, 5, 6, 2, and 5 years old. What is the mode of the ages?

_____

7. Karen earned scores of 4, 5, 5, 6, 5, 6, and 5 in a diving competition. What is the median score?

_____

8. Which of the following can be used to show how spread out a set of data is? Circle all that apply.

      mean   median   mode   range

9. Which of the following is calculated by using addition and division? Circle all that apply.

      mean   median   mode   range

Prediction

Basketball Practice

Directions: Use the trend graph to answer the questions on the page 62.

Bryan has been practicing his free throws during the past 5 weeks. His weekly free throw percentage is shown in the trend graph.

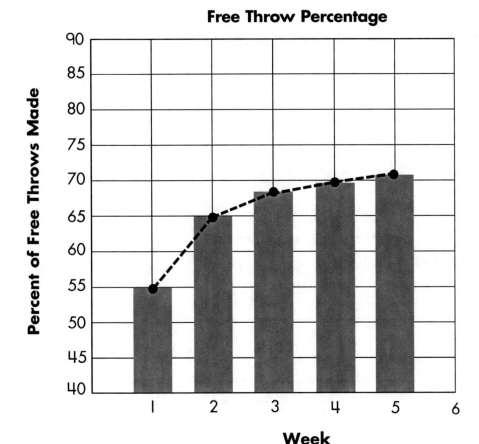

Prediction

Name _____ Date _____

Basketball Practice

Directions: Use the trend graph on page 61 to answer each question.

1. Describe the shape of the data in the trend graph.

   _____

   _____

2. How would you describe Bryan's weekly progress? Is he getting better or worse? Explain.

   _____

   _____

3. Do you think Bryan's free throw percentage will be greater than or less than 70% after 6 weeks of practice? Explain.

   _____

   _____

DO MORE

Between which 2 weeks did Bryan's free throw percentage increase the most? How much did it increase during this time?

Prediction Name _____ Date _____

Snow Day

Directions: Use the pictograph to answer the questions on page 64.

Hamilton Elementary School had a snow day. The pictograph shows the number of sled riding trips four friends took down a hill.

Sled Ride Trips Down the Hill

Timothy	🛷 🛷 🛷 🛷
Adrianne	🛷 🛷 🛷 🛷 🛷
Jennifer	🛷 🛷 🛷
Robert	🛷 🛷 🛷 🛷 🛷 🛷

Key: 🛷 = 2 trips

Prediction Name _____ Date _____

Snow Day

Directions: Use the pictograph on page 63 to answer each question.

1. What is the average number of sled ride trips taken by the four students?

   _____

2. Which student took the most sled ride trips down the hill?

   _____

3. Which student took the fewest sled ride trips down the hill?

   _____

4. Which student took twice as many sled ride trips as Jennifer?

   _____

5. Adrianne says that Robert took more sled ride trips than Timothy and Jennifer combined. Do you agree or disagree with this statement? Explain.

   _____

   _____

Prediction   Name _____ Date _____

Arts and Crafts

Directions: Use the bar graph to answer the questions on page 66.

The students in Mr. Ulrich's art class were asked to vote on their favorite class activity. The results are shown in the bar graph.

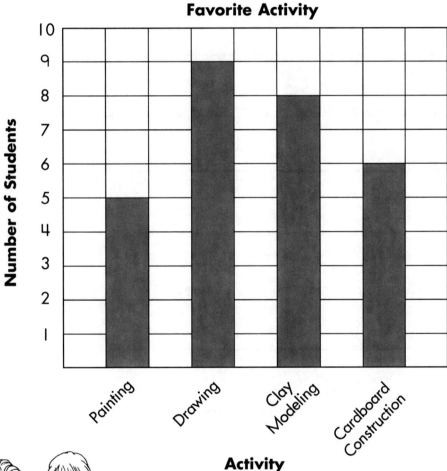

Prediction

Name _____ Date _____

Arts and Crafts

Directions: Tell whether you agree or disagree with each statement. Circle each answer and explain how you reached your conclusion.

1. The most popular activity was drawing. agree disagree

   _____

   _____

2. The least popular activity was clay modeling. agree disagree

   _____

   _____

3. Drawing was twice as popular as painting. agree disagree

   _____

   _____

DO MORE

Write another statement about the data in the bar graph. Trade your statement with a classmate and see if you agree with each other's statement.

Prediction

Growth Rate

Directions: Ricky is testing whether or not plant fertilizer has any effect on a plant's growth rate. He used the fertilizer during the third week. Make a line graph of the data. Then answer the questions on page 68.

Week	Height (cm)
1	8
2	10
3	15
4	18
5	20

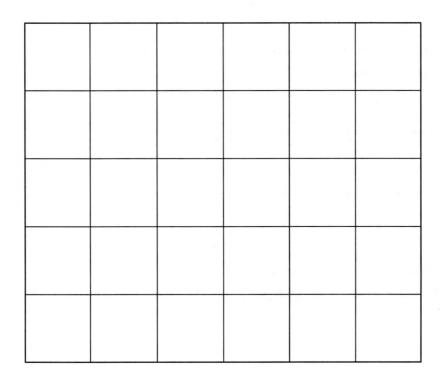

Prediction   Name _____   Date _____

Growth Rate

Directions: Use the line graph from page 67 to answer each question.

1. Describe the shape of the data in the line graph. How would you describe the growth of the plant each week?

   _____

   _____

2. Between which weeks did the height of the plant increase the most?

   _____

3. Based on the line graph, what conclusion would you draw about the use of the plant fertilizer? Explain.

   _____

   _____

THINK

If the fertilizer had not been used during week 3, how many centimeters do you think the plant would have grown during this week? Explain.

Prediction Name _____ Date _____

The Dragonfly

Directions: The dragonfly is the fastest insect in the world. A scientist recorded the top flying speed of several dragonflies. Use the line plot to answer each question.

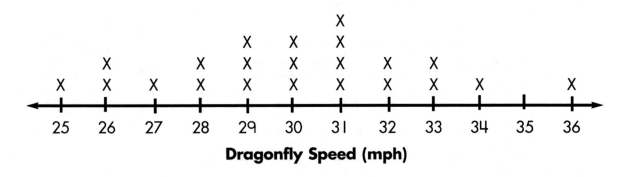

Dragonfly Speed (mph)

1. Describe the shape of the data on the line plot.

   _____

2. What is the fastest speed shown in the line plot?

   _____

3. Michael says that the range of the data is 10 miles per hour. Do you agree with this statement? Explain.

   _____

4. Geoff claims that the mode of the data is 31 miles per hour. Do you agree with this statement? Explain.

   _____

Prediction

Name _____ Date _____

Rattlesnakes

Directions: The table shows the lengths of different species of rattlesnakes. Make a bar graph of the data. Then answer the questions on page 71.

Rattlesnake	Length (feet)
Eastern Diamondback	7
Mojave	4
Timber	6
Pigmy	2
Canebrake	6

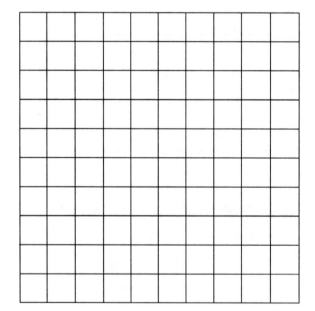

THINK

How does a bar graph make it easier to compare the lengths of the rattlesnakes? Explain.

Prediction

Name _____ Date _____

Rattlesnakes

Directions: Use the bar graph from the page 70 to answer each question.

1. What is the shortest rattlesnake shown on the graph? What is the longest?

   _____

2. Nick claims that an Eastern Diamondback is twice as long as Mojave rattlesnake. Do you agree with this statement? Explain.

   _____

   _____

3. What conclusion can you draw about the length of a Timber rattlesnake compared to the length of a Pigmy rattlesnake?

   _____

   _____

4. Write a statement about how the length of an Eastern Diamondback rattlesnake compares to the lengths of the other snakes listed.

   _____

   _____

Prediction

Name _____ Date _____

A Puzzling Problem

Directions: Use the tally chart to make a line plot. Then answer the questions on page 73.

Teams at an academic competition worked on a math puzzle. The time each team took to complete the puzzle is shown in the tally chart.

Time Needed to Solve a Puzzle		
Time (minutes)	**Tally**	**Number**
2	|	1
4		0
6		0
8		0
10	||	2
14	||||	4
16	⊞	5
18	||	2
20	|||	3
22	|	1

Prediction   Name _____ Date _____

A Puzzling Problem

Directions: Make a line plot of the data from page 72 in the space below. Then answer each question.

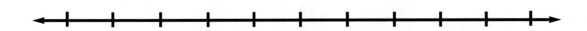

1. Describe the shape of the data in the line plot. Does it look like a mountain peak or a valley?

   _____

2. Just by looking at the line plot, what would you say is the mean time? Explain.

   _____

3. Are there any outliers in the data? If so, name them.

   _____

True or False

Directions: Use the bar graph to answer the true or false questions on page 75.

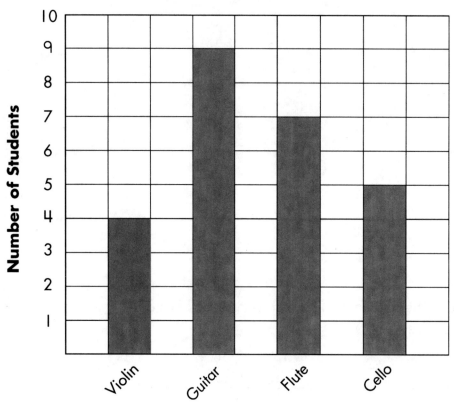

Favorite Musical Instrument

Prediction   Name _____   Date _____

True or False

Directions: Use the bar graph on page 74 to answer each question.
Circle true or false.

1. The most popular instrument is the guitar.   true   false

2. The least popular instrument is the flute.   true   false

3. The guitar is three times as popular as the violin.   true   false

4. As many students voted for the guitar as voted for
   the violin and cello combined.   true   false

5. If this data is representative of all music students,
   then 20 out of 100 students would likely vote for
   the violin.   true   false

6. If this data is representative of all music students,
   then 60 out of 300 students would likely vote for
   the cello.   true   false

DO MORE

Use the bar graph to draw a conclusion about the instruments.
Ask a classmate if your conclusion is true or false.

Prediction   Name _____ Date _____

Let's Go to the Beach

Directions: The line plot shows how far several students live from the beach. Use the line plot to answer each question.

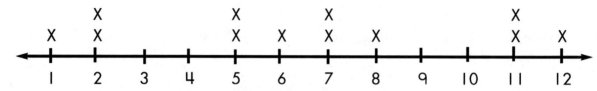

Distance from the Beach (km)

1. What is the farthest distance that any of the students lives from the beach?

   _____

2. Mario claims that 5 students live at least 7 kilometers from the beach. Do you agree or disagree? Explain.

   _____

3. Andrea thinks that only 3 students live within 2 kilometers of the beach. Do you agree or disagree? Explain.

   _____

THINK

   How many clusters, or groups, of data are there on the line plot?

Prediction   Name _____ Date _____

Create Your Own Problems

1. Write a word problem about making an incorrect statement from a data display.

2. Draw a bar graph to represent a data set. Make a statement about the data. Exchange statements with a classmate and decide if you each agree with them.

3. Write a question that involves drawing a conclusion from a set of data.

4. Write a problem that involves graphing data from a tally chart. Draw a conclusion from the data display.

Prediction

Check Your Skills

Use the line graph to answer questions 1 – 2.

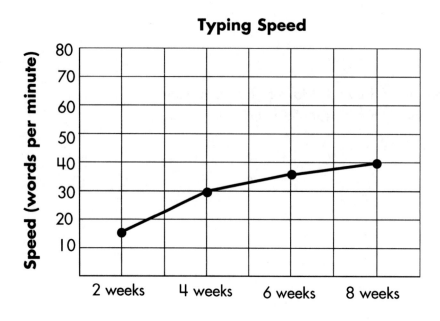

1. What conclusion can you draw about typing speed and the amount of time spent practicing?

   _____

2. Do you think a person will type more or fewer than 40 words per minute after 10 weeks of practice? Explain.

   _____

Prediction

Check Your Skills (cont.)

David recorded the number of strikes that he rolled in several games of bowling. Use the line plot to answer questions 3 – 6.

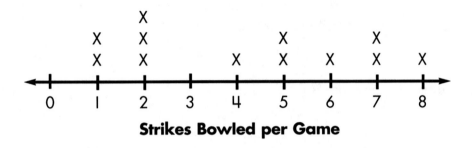

3. How many games of bowling are shown in the line plot?

_____

4. David said that he rolled at least 4 strikes in 6 of the games. Do you agree or disagree with this statement? Explain.

_____

5. How many times did David roll 2 strikes in a game? How does this compare to the number of times he rolled 8 strikes? Explain.

_____

6. In how many games did David roll less than 3 strikes?

_____

Probability

Name _____ Date _____

Possible Verses Impossible

An event that can never occur is **impossible**.

An event that might occur is **possible**.

Directions: Tell whether each event is impossible or possible.

1. It will snow when the outside temperature is 85°F. _____

2. You will roll a number less than 4 on a number cube. _____

3. Megan's gym class will play volleyball this year. _____

4. Tomorrow will be 25 hours long. _____

5. Christopher will pass a limousine on the way to school today. _____

6. A deer will learn to read. _____

DO MORE

Give another example of a possible event and an example of an impossible event.

Probability — Name _____ Date _____

Things That Are Certain

An event that will definitely occur is **certain**.

Directions: Tell whether each event is impossible, possible, or certain.

1. There will be 60 seconds in the next minute.

   _____

2. Karl will flip heads 3 times in a row with a quarter.   _____

3. The day after Wednesday is Thursday.   _____

4. Jenny will roll a 7 on a number cube labeled 1 to 6.   _____

5. Mary will score the highest grade in her class.   _____

6. A baseball team with a losing record will win a game.   _____

THINK

Hector says that he will certainly score the most points in tomorrow's basketball game. Do you agree or disagree with this statement?

Probability

Name _____ Date _____

Events in Your Life

Directions: Follow each instruction.

1. Think of an event in everyday life that is possible. Sketch a picture of the event.

2. Think of an event that is impossible. Sketch a picture of the event.

3. Think of an event in everyday life that is certain. Sketch a picture of the event.

DO MORE

Share your sketches with a classmate. Ask him or her to decide which event is possible, impossible, or certain.

Probability

Likely and Unlikely Events

If there is a good chance that an event will occur, then it is a **likely** event.

If an event is possible but has a small chance of occurring, then it is an **unlikely** event.

Directions: Tell whether each event is likely or unlikely.

1. Lori will flip tails with a nickel 20 times in a row. _____

2. The tree Amy planted last spring will grow this year. _____

3. You will travel to Antarctica next month. _____

4. It is raining somewhere in the world right now. _____

5. You will be awake at 3:30 P.M. next Wednesday. _____

6. The date of Thanksgiving day will be in the mid-twenties. _____

7. You will pass a school bus sometime within the next week. _____

THINK

Two events that have the same chance of occurring are **equally likely**.
Give an example of two equally likely events.

On a Roll

Directions: Suppose Megan rolls a number cube one time. Which event is more likely? Circle A or B. If the events are equally likely, circle both A and B.

A   rolling a 5

B   rolling a number less than 3

A   rolling an odd number

B   rolling an even number

A   rolling either a 3 or a 5

B   rolling a whole number

A   rolling an odd number

B   rolling a number greater than 4

Probability　　　Name _____ Date _____

More Events

Directions: Give an example of a likely event, an unlikely event, and two events that are equally likely.
Give each example in the context given.

1. likely event in sports

   _____

   _____

2. unlikely event in school

   _____

   _____

3. equally likely event in shopping

   _____

   _____

THINK

Suppose a student is selected at random from a group of 8 girls and 6 boys. Will that student likely be a girl or a boy? Explain.

Probability Name _____ Date _____

Outcomes

A possible result of an event is an **outcome**.

For example, if you flip a coin, the two possible outcomes are heads and tails.

Directions: List all possible outcomes for each event.

1. selecting a coin from a piggy bank that contains pennies, nickels, dimes, and quarters

2. spinning the spinner at the right

THINK

Think of an event that has 10 possible outcomes. Describe that event.

Probability — Name _____ Date _____

Tree Diagrams

The set of all possible outcomes of an event is the **sample space**.

You can use a **tree diagram** to help you find the sample space of more complicated events.

Directions: The fourth graders will choose between kickball, four square, and soccer for gym class. They will either play indoors or outdoors. Use the tree diagram to answer the questions on page 88.

Location   **Activity**   **Outcome**

indoors
- kickball —— indoors, kickball
- four square —— indoors, four square
- soccer —— indoors, soccer

outdoors
- kickball —— outdoors, kickball
- four square —— outdoors, four square
- soccer —— outdoors, soccer

Published by Instructional Fair. Copyright protected.   0-7424-2994-6 *Using the Standards: Data Analysis and Probability*

Probability

Name _____ Date _____

Tree Diagrams

Directions: Use the tree diagram on page 87 to answer each question.

1. How many choices for the location are there?

   _____

2. How many choices for the activity are there?

   _____

3. How many outcomes are there in the sample space?

   _____

4. What would the number of outcomes be if the students could also choose baseball as an activity?

   _____

THINK

When you multiply the number of choices for the location and the number of choices for the activity, the product equals the number of outcomes in the sample space. Do you think this is always the case with tree diagrams? Explain.

Probability

Name _____ Date _____

Make a Tree Diagram

Directions: Make a tree diagram. Use the tree diagram to answer each question.

The cafeteria has two different sizes of drink: regular and large. Students can get milk, lemonade, apple juice, or grape juice in either size. Make a tree diagram to show the sample space.

Size **Flavor** **Outcome**

1. How many outcomes are there in the sample space? _____

2. How many outcomes would there be if there were three different sizes instead of two? _____

Probability

Name _____ Date _____

Predicting Outcomes

A **prediction** is a guess about how likely or unlikely an event is.

Directions: Read each situation and make a prediction.

1. There are 8 purple marbles, 5 green marbles, and 3 red marbles in a bag. Timmy picks one marble at random. What color do you think it will be? Explain.

   _____

   _____

2. Andrew's sister is reading a book that is 24 pages long. Of the pages, 20 of them have an illustration. Suppose you randomly turn to a page in the book. Do you think it will have an illustration? Explain.

   _____

   _____

DO MORE

Describe a situation that happens during the school day which has at least two possible outcomes. Make a prediction about it.

Probability

Experiments

You can test a prediction by conducting an **experiment**.

Directions: Follow the directions to conduct an experiment.

1. Place 4 red crayons and 2 blue crayons in a box or a bag. Predict which color crayon you are more likely to pull out of the box or bag.

   _____

2. Test your prediction. Pull out a crayon and record its color in the tally chart. Then replace the crayon. Repeat this experiment 30 times.

Color	Tally	Number
Blue		
Red		

3. Did the experiment agree with your prediction? Explain why or why not.

   _____

THINK

Are the two possible outcomes in the experiment equally likely? Explain.

Probability

Name _____ Date _____

Roll the Dice

Directions: When you roll a number cube, there are 6 possible outcomes. Follow the directions to conduct an experiment.

1. Is each outcome equally likely to occur? Can you predict which number will occur most often if you roll the number cube 60 times? Explain.

   _____

2. Test your prediction. Roll a number cube 60 times and record the results in the table.

Outcome	Number of Rolls
1	
2	
3	
4	
5	
6	

3. Were the results of the experiment what you expected? Explain why or why not.

   _____

THINK

Suppose you flip a coin 20 times. How many times would you expect to flip heads? Explain.

Probability

Conduct an Experiment

Directions: Design and conduct your own experiment using two different kinds of blocks, coins, cards, or buttons.

1. Describe your experiment. What outcomes are possible?

   _____

2. Are the outcomes equally likely? Explain.

   _____

3. Make a prediction about the outcome of your experiment.

   _____

4. Perform the experiment at least 20 times. Record the results in a tally chart.

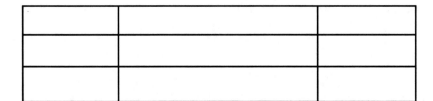

5. Did the experiment agree with your prediction? Explain why or why not.

   _____

Probability

Is That Fair?

A game is **fair** if each person playing the game has the same chance of winning.

Directions: Edward, Megan, and David are playing a game using the spinner. Tell who has the best chance of winning each game. Explain.

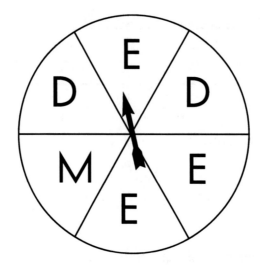

1. The players take turns spinning the spinner. Each person gets 1 point if they spin the first letter of their name. They play to 10 points.

   _____

2. The players take turns spinning the spinner. Each person gets 1 point if they spin a letter in their name. They play to 10 points.

   _____

3. The players take turns spinning the spinner. Each person gets 2 points if they spin a vowel, and they each lose 1 point if they spin a consonant. They play to 15 points.

   _____

Probability

Name _____ Date _____

Designing a Fair Game

Directions: Design a fair game using the spinner below.

1. Describe the rules of your game. Be sure to include how many points it takes to win.

   _____

   _____

2. Play the game with your classmates.

DO MORE

Describe a set of rules that makes it an unfair game.

Probability

Probability

The **probability** of an event is the chance that it will occur. Probabilities are often expressed as fractions. The probability of an event ranges from 0 (impossible) to 1 (certain).

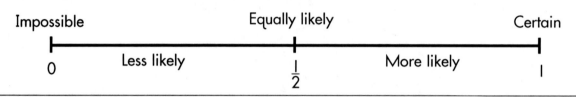

Directions: Answer each question.

1. Suppose the probability of pulling a blue chip from a bag is $\frac{1}{4}$, and the probability of pulling a red chip is $\frac{1}{2}$. Which event is more likely? Explain.

   _____

2. Kendra rolls two number cubes while playing a board game. The probability that both number cubes show an odd number is $\frac{1}{4}$. The probability that both cubes show the same number is $\frac{1}{6}$. Which event is more likely? Explain.

   _____

3. A cookie jar contains 6 sugar cookies, 4 chocolate chip cookies, and 8 peanut butter cookies. Which type of cookie has the greatest probability of being selected? Explain.

   _____

THINK

Probability is usually expressed as a fraction, but it can be written in different ways. Name two other ways that probability can be expressed.

The Probability Formula

To calculate the probability of an event, use the following formula.

Probability of an event = $\dfrac{\text{number of favorable outcomes}}{\text{number of possible outcomes}}$

Directions: Find the probability of each event using the formula. Express each answer as a fraction in reduced form.

There are 12 students in the school play: 4 third graders, 6 fourth graders, and 2 fifth graders. Suppose one of these students is chosen at random.

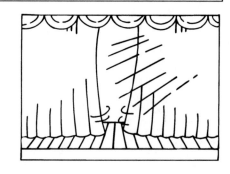

1. What is the probability that the student will be a third grader?

   _____

2. What is the probability that the student will be a fourth grader?

   _____

3. What is the probability that the student will be a fifth grader?

   _____

THINK

Which event is most likely? How does the probability of this event compare to each of the probabilities of the other two events?

Probability and Spinners

Directions: Find the probability of each event. Express each answer as a reduced fraction.

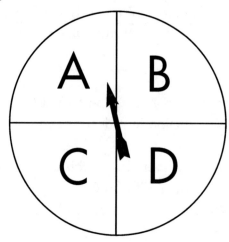

1. spinning the letter B _____

2. spinning a vowel _____

3. spinning a consonant _____

4. spinning the letter B or the letter D _____

5. spinning the letter A, the letter B, or the letter C _____

6. not spinning a consonant _____

THINK

 What should the sum of the probabilities in questions 3 and 6 be?

Pick a Card

Directions: Nancy has 7 letter cards face down on her desk. She picks 1 card at random. Find the probability of each event.

1. picking a card with a T

   _____

2. picking a card with an M or an O

   _____

3. picking a card with a vowel

   _____

4. picking a card with a consonant

   _____

5. picking a card that has a letter made only with curves

   _____

6. picking a card that has a letter from her name

   _____

THINK

What letter could you add to the end of the word OUTCOME (and still have a word) so that picking a vowel would have the same probability as picking a consonant?

Probability   Name _____   Date _____

A Decision-Making Spinner

Directions: Every morning Julie likes to eat a piece of fruit. She spins the spinner to decide which kind of fruit she will eat. The spinner shows 3 bananas, 2 apples, and 1 peach. Use the spinner to answer each question.

1. What is the probability that Julie will eat an apple this morning?   _____

2. What is the probability that Julie will eat a peach tomorrow morning?   _____

3. What is the probability that Julie will eat a banana Friday morning?   _____

4. What is the probability that Julie will not eat an apple one morning?   _____

5. One week Julie did not buy bananas. Each time the spinner landed on banana she would spin again. Predict how many times Julie had to spin again during that week.   _____

THINK

How many bananas would you expect Julie to eat over a period of 10 mornings? Explain.

Probability

Pizza Parlor

Directions: The Pizza Parlor restaurant offers 2 different kinds of crust: hand-tossed and thin crust. Customers can choose from 5 different toppings:

    pepperoni   mushrooms
    green peppers   onions
    sausage

Make a tree diagram to show all of the possible 1-topping pizzas offered at the Pizza Parlor.

Then use the tree diagram to answer the questions on page 102.

Crust   **Topping**   **Outcome**

Pizza Parlor

Directions: Suppose Joseph picks a 1-topping pizza at random. Use your tree diagram from page 101 to answer each question.

1. How many different 1-topping pizzas are available? _____

2. What is the probability that Joseph will select a hand-tossed pizza with pepperoni? _____

3. What is the probability that Joseph will select a thin crust pizza with green peppers? _____

4. What is the probability that the pizza Joseph selects will be a hand-tossed pizza? _____

5. What is the probability that the pizza Joseph selects will have sausage? _____

6. What is the probability that Joseph will select a deep dish pizza with anchovies? _____

THINK

Explain how tree diagrams help you find probability.

Probability Name _____ Date _____

Getting Dressed

Directions: Use the tree diagram to answer each question.

Mr. Chow is deciding what to wear to school today. Suppose he picks an outfit at random from 2 different kinds of pants and 4 different color shirts.

Pants	Color Shirt	Outcome
jeans	red	jeans, red shirt
	yellow	jeans, yellow shirt
	blue	jeans, blue shirt
	white	jeans, white shirt
slacks	red	slacks, red shirt
	yellow	slacks, yellow shirt
	blue	slacks, blue shirt
	white	slacks, white shirt

1. What is the probability that Mr. Chow will wear jeans and a white shirt? _____

2. What is the probability that Mr. Chow will wear slacks? _____

3. What is the probability that Mr. Chow will wear a yellow shirt? _____

A Probability Riddle

Directions: Answer each question. Circle the letter of the correct answer. Then use your answers to complete the riddle on page 105.

1. A possible result of an event is called an _____.

    H experiment   **R** outcome

2. The _____ is the set of all possible outcomes of an event.

    C tree diagram   **Y** sample space

3. An event that will always occur is _____.

    P certain   **F** likely

4. A(n) _____ event might occur.

    O possible   **S** impossible

5. You can conduct an _____ to test a prediction.

    I event   **B** experiment

6. A(n) _____ game is one where each player has an equal chance of winning.

    L fair   **T** unfair

Probability

Name _____ Date _____

A Probability Riddle

Directions: Use your answers from page 104 to solve the riddle. Place the letter of each correct answer in the corresponding blank. One of the blanks has been filled for you.

Riddle: William asked Mrs. Ingram if he will have any math homework to do tonight. What was her response?

__ __ __ __ A __ __ __
3 1 4 5   5 6 2

Probability   Name _____   Date _____

Create Your Own Problems

1. Write a question about likely and unlikely events.

2. Write a question about an impossible event.

3. Write a question about using a tree diagram to list all of the possible outcomes of an event.

4. Write a word problem about predicting the outcome of an event and testing the prediction with an experiment.

5. Write a word problem about using a tree diagram to list a sample space of an event and finding the probability of one of the possible outcomes.

Check Your Skills

Tell whether each event is likely, unlikely, impossible, or certain.

1. Kyle will walk on the ceiling tonight. _____

2. Martin will stay awake for 3 days in a row. _____

3. If Valerie throws a rock up into the air, it will return to Earth. _____

4. Megan will have social studies homework next school year. _____

Tim spins the spinner at the right 1 time.

5. List all the possible outcomes.

   _____

6. Which number has the greatest probability of being spun?

   _____

7. What is the probability of spinning a 1?

   _____

Probability Name _____ Date _____

Check Your Skills (cont.)

A deli offers sandwiches on 3 different kinds of bread:
   wheat   rye   white

The choices of meat are:
   turkey   ham   tuna salad

Suppose Tonya chooses a sandwich at random.

8. Make a tree diagram of all the possible outcomes.

   Bread   **Meat**   **Outcome**

9. How many different outcomes are possible? _____

10. What is the probability that Tonya will order a turkey sandwich on wheat bread? _____

11. What is the probability that Tonya will order tuna salad? _____

Post Test

Make a pictograph of the data in the tally chart. Use the graph to answer questions 1 – 3.

Number of Books Read Last Summer		
Student	**Tally**	**Number**
Jorge	卌 I	6
Stewart	IIII	4
Melissa	卌 III	8

1. Which student read the most books last summer? _____

2. How many fewer books did Stewart read than Jorge? _____

3. How many more books did Melissa read than Stewart? _____

Name _____ Date _____

Post Test (cont.)

Andy's mom is buying a table and a couch for the family room. Use the tree diagram to answer questions 4 – 6.

Table	Couch Color	Outcome
oak	green	oak table, green couch
	black	oak table, black couch
	beige	oak table, beige couch
	white	oak table, white couch
cedar	green	cedar table, green couch
	black	cedar table, black couch
	beige	cedar table, beige couch
	white	cedar table, white couch

4. How many outcomes are there in the sample space? _____

5. What is the probability that Andy's mom will buy an oak table and a beige couch? _____

6. What is the probability that Andy's mom will buy a cedar table? _____

7. If Andy's mom also had the choice of 2 colors for couch pads, how would that impact the number of outcomes in the sample space?

_____

Answer Key

Pretest 7-8
1. Mandy
2. 7
3. 2
4. 7
5. mean: 2; median: 2; mode: 1, 3; range: 2
6. 6

buttermilk — maple — buttermilk, maple
buttermilk — lite maple — buttermilk, lite maple

whole wheat — maple — whole wheat, maple
whole wheat — lite maple — whole wheat, lite maple

blueberry — maple — blueberry, maple
blueberry — lite maple — blueberry, lite maple

7. They are all equal. There is $\frac{1}{3}$ chance for each kind of pancake.
8. $\frac{1}{6}$

Collecting Information 9
Dog, |||| |||
Cat, |||
Fish, ||||
Bird, ||

THINK: So you can quickly mark down responses as your sample answers the survey.

Ask Your Classmates 10
Tally charts will vary, but will look similar to chart shown on page 9.
THINK: Answers will vary.

Samples 11
1. no
2. yes
3. no
4. no

Match the Sample 12
1. customers at a local movie rental store
2. customers in a pet supply store in your town
3. customers at the local auto dealership
4. shoppers coming out of a local grocery in town
5. customers at the local Chinese restaurant

THINK: You will not get accurate survey results.

Bias 13
1. Answers will vary. Sample answer: Only Spanish and German students were surveyed. There are other languages.
   Answers will vary. Sample answer: Survey 50 students who have taken a foreign language.
2. Answers will vary. Sample answer: Only students eating pretzels were surveyed.
   Answers will vary. Sample answer: Survey fourth graders who bought a snack for one day.

Facts Verses Opinions 14
1. fact
2. opinion
3. opinion
4. opinion
5. fact
6. fact

DO MORE: Answers will vary. Sample answers are given. fact - The telephone pole is 168 inches tall. opinion - The telephone pole is very tall.

Surveys in Everyday Life 15
1-5. Answers will vary.

Create a Tally Chart 16
Tally charts will vary.
THINK: Answers will vary.

A Crossword Puzzle 17-18
Across
2. sample
3. bias
6. tally
7. data

Down
1. opinion
4. survey
5. fact

Answer Key

Pictographs 19
1. Alfonso
2. 2
3. 3

THINK: half of a book

Line Plots 20
1. 25
2. 4
3. 11
4. 7

DO MORE: 6

Bar Graphs 21–22
1. 25
2. building campfire
3. pitching tent
4. 3
5. 16

THINK: 29

Trend Graphs 23–24
1. Tuesday and Wednesday
2. Thursday
3. 23
4. 3
5. Tuesday and Wednesday

THINK: Answers will vary. Sample answer: bad weather

Line Graphs 25–26
1. 0.4 cm
2. 0.6 cm
3. 2 and 3
4. 1 and 2
5. 0.6 cm

Paper Route 27
Pictographs will vary. Sample pictograph is shown.

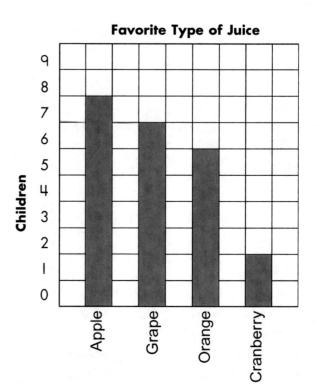

Make a Bar Graph 28
Graphs will vary. Sample graph is shown.

Answer Key

Swimming Laps 29
Line plots will vary. Sample line plot is shown.

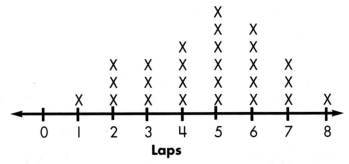

THINK: The numbers along the number line had to be the number of laps because they were sequential. That made the number of students represented by each X.

Let it Snow! 30
Graphs will vary. Sample graph is shown.

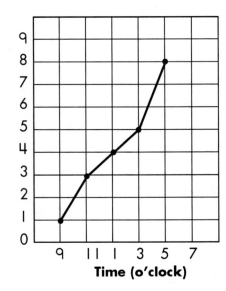

Make a Trend Graph 31
Trend graphs will vary. Sample graph is shown.

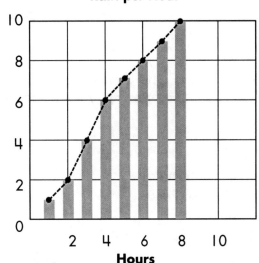

Tell a Story 32
1–4. Stories will vary.
THINK: Answers will vary.

Display Your Story 33
1–4. Graphs will vary, but will look similar to each type presented on pages 27 – 31.

Choose the Better Display 34
The bar graph is the better display.

Which Type of Graph? 35
1. trend graph
2. line plot
3. bar graph

THINK: yes; Question 1 can be a bar graph.

All Kinds of Graphs 36
1. bar graph   2. line graph
3. pictograph   4. line plot

Answer Key

Create Your Own Problems 37
Answers will vary.

Check Your Skills 38–39
1. Answers will vary.
2. Answers will vary.
3. Graphs will vary, but Christian solved 4 puzzles, Vicky solved 3 puzzles, and Alfonso solved 6 puzzles.
4. 3.5 feet
5. 0.5 feet
6. Friday and Saturday
7. Thursday and Friday

The Mean 40
1. 358
2. $65
3. 453
4. 7.8

THINK: Answers will vary. Sample answer: They add all temperatures on that date and then divide by the number of temperatures.

Means in the World 41
1. 48.75 mph
2. 1,438 feet
3. 251.2 feet
4. 5,673 miles

Middle of the Road 42
1. 15
2. 714
3. 324
4. 5

THINK: The same way. It is the number in the middle.

Find the Median 43
1. 21, 28, ⑤③, 55, 62
2. 236, 359, ④③②, 537, 752
3. 16, 23, 33, ③⑤, 47, 58, 96
4. 212, 236, 258, ②⑥③, 367, 469, 674
5. 43, 77, 79, ①⑤⑤, 168, 182, 218
6. 8, 10, 11, ⑭, 16, 22, 25

THINK: Take the 2 middle numbers, add them, and divide by 2.

Medians of the World 44
1. 80 decibels
2. 17.5 years
3. 81 stories
4. 185 calories

The Mode 45
1. 5
2. 2

THINK: line plot; Explanations will vary, but may include that a line plot shows the mode because it is the tallest stack of Xs.

Create a Data Set 46
Data sets will vary. Sample data sets are given.
1. 8, 6, 3, 2, 1
2. 7, 2, 1, 3, 6
3. 1, 11, 14, 7, 14, 9
4. 12, 6, 7, 8, 6

DO MORE: Data sets will vary. Sample data set is 21, 18, 13, 14, 13, 7, 5

The Range 47
1. 66
2. 433
3. 143
4. 643
5. 79
6. 347

THINK: The range tells you how spread out the data are. Explanations will vary.

Home on the Range 48
1. 7
2. 6
3. 8

Compare the Graphs 49–50
1. Mr. Wilson's class
2. Mr. Wilson's class - 11, Miss Clark's class - 11
3. Mr. Wilson's class - 8, Miss Clark's class - 6
4. Mr. Wilson's class - 5, Miss Clark's class - 6
5. For Mr. Wilson's class the range tells that the work of the students was more spread out. Some students worked harder than others. For Miss Clark's class the range tells that the work of students was more evenly distributed.

THINK: Mr. Wilson's class; yes; The data is more spread out.

Answer Key

A Helping Hand 51
mean: 8; median: 8; mode: no mode; range: 2

Cafeteria Duty 52
mean: 20; mode: 20; range: 10

Way Out There 53
1. 21
2. 5

THINK: yes; Explanations will vary, but may include that there could be an outlier on the greater end of data values and one on the lesser end of the data values.

One Big Bird 54
1. 16
2. 5 feet
3. no; The difference from one data value to the next is only 1.

Sketch the Plots .55
Line plots will vary. Sample line plots are shown.

1st Period Grades

3rd Period Grades

DO MORE: Answers will vary.

Know the Terms .56
1. mode
2. median
3. range
4. mean
5. outlier
6. Data

Word Search 57

DO MORE: average

Create Your Own Problems 58
Answers will vary.

Check Your Skills 59–60
1. 11
2. 8
3. 12
4. yes; 5
5. 10
6. 5
7. 5
8. range
9. mean and median when the data set has an even number of elements

Basketball Practice 61–62
1. Descriptions will vary. Sample description: left side of an arch
2. better; The trend line is increasing.
3. greater than 70%; After 5 weeks he has already reached 70%, and he is steadily improving.

DO MORE: weeks 1 and 2; 10%

Answer Key

Snow Day 63–64
1. 9
2. Robert
3. Jennifer
4. Robert
5. disagree; Robert took 12 trips. Timothy and Jennifer took 14 trips combined.

Arts and Crafts 65–66

Explanations will vary. Sample explanations are given.
1. agree; The bar for drawing is the tallest.
2. disagree; The bar for clay modeling is not the shortest.
3. disagree; Painting had 5 votes. Drawing had 9 votes. Twice 5 is not 9.

DO MORE: Statements will vary.

Growth Rate 67–68

Graphs will vary. Sample graph is shown.

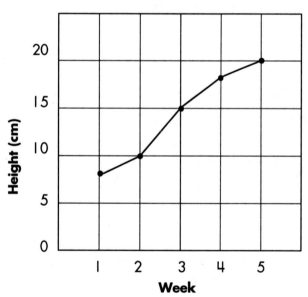

1. Answers will vary, but should mention an increasing trend.
2. 2 and 3
3. Answers will vary. Sample answer: The week in which the fertilizer was used caused the plant to grow the most.

THINK: Answers will vary, but should be less than 5 cm.

The Dragonfly 69
1. Answers will vary, but should mention a mountain peak.
2. 36 mph
3. no; Answers will vary. Sample answer: 11 mph is the range
4. yes; Answers will vary. Sample answer: 31 had the tallest stack of Xs.

Rattlesnakes 70–71

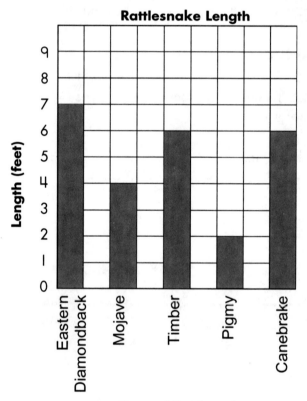

THINK: It is easy to look at the heights of the bars.
1. Pigmy, Eastern Diamondback
2. no; Answers will vary. Sample answer: Mojave is 4 feet. Eastern Diamondback is 7 feet. Twice 4 feet is not 7 feet.
3. Answers will vary. Sample answer: Timber rattlesnake is 3 times longer than Pigmy.
4. Answers will vary. Sample answer: The Eastern Diamondback is the longest rattlesnake.

Answer Key

A Puzzling Problem 72-73

```
                    X
                X   X
                X   X
            X   X   X       X
        X   X   X   X   X   X
    X       X   X   X   X   X   X
  ←—+—+—+—+—+—+—+—+—+—+—+—→
    2   4   6   8  10  12  14  16  18  20  22
         Time Needed to Solve a Puzzle
```

1. mountain peak
2. about 15; Answers will vary. Sample answer: You cannot say exactly what the mean is but a cluster from 14 to 16 indicates the mean will be within that range.
3. yes, 2

True or False 74–75

1. true   2. false   3. false
4. true   5. false   6. true

DO MORE: Answers will vary. Sample answer: More than twice as many chose the guitar over the cello.

Let's Go to the Beach 76

1. 12 km
2. agree; Six students live at least 7 km from the beach.
3. agree; Two students live 2 km from the beach and 1 student lives 1 km from the beach.

THINK: 3

Create Your Own Problems 77

Answers will vary.

Check Your Skills 78–79

1. Answers will vary. Possible answer: As practice increases the number of words per minutes increases.
2. more; Answers will vary. Possible answer: The speed has been increasing and at 8 weeks it is already 40 words per minute. So, after 10 weeks, the speed should be more than 40 words per minute.

3. 12
4. agree; He rolled 4 strikes in 1 game, 5 strikes in 2 games, 6 strikes in 1 game, 7 strikes in 2 games, and 8 strikes in 1 game. So, he rolled at least 4 strikes in 7 games.
5. 10; On the line plots the Xs on every number 2 or greater need to be counted. He only bowled 8 strikes in 1 game. So, he rolled 2 strikes in 9 more games than he rolled 8 strikes.
6. 5

Possible Verses Impossible 80

1. impossible   2. possible
3. possible   4. impossible
5. possible   6. impossible

DO MORE: Answers will vary.

Things That Are Certain 81

1. certain   2. possible
3. certain   4. impossible
5. possible   6. possible

THINK: disagree

Events in Your Life 82

1-3. Answers will vary.

DO MORE: Answers will vary.

Likely and Unlikely Events 83

1. unlikely   2. likely
3. unlikely   4. likely
5. likely   6. likely
7. likely

THINK: Answers will vary. Sample answer: flipping a penny and it landing on heads or tails.

On a Roll 84

B; A and B; B; A

Answer Key

More Events 85
   1–3. Answers will vary.
THINK: girl; There are more girls in the group than boys.

Outcomes 86
   1. penny, nickel, dime, quarter
   2. 1, 2, 3, 4, 5, 6, 7, 8
THINK: Answers will vary. Sample answer: spinner labeled 1 to 10.

Tree Diagrams 87–88
   1. 2   **2.** 3
   3. 6   **4.** 8
THINK: yes; Answers will vary.

Make a Tree Diagram 89

regular
- milk — regular, milk
- lemonade — regular, lemonade
- apple juice — regular, apple juice
- grape juice — regular, grape juice

large
- milk — large, milk
- lemonade — large, lemonade
- apple juice — large, apple juice
- grape juice — large, grape juice

   1. 8   **2.** 12

Predicting Outcomes 90
   1. purple; There are more purple marbles.
   2. yes; There are more pages with an illustration.
DO MORE: Answers will vary.

Experiments 91
   1. red
   2. Experiment results will vary.
   3. Answers will vary.
THINK: no; There are not an equal number of red and blue crayons.

Roll the Dice 92
   1. yes; Each outcome should occur an equal number of times.
   2. Experiment results will vary.
   3. Answers will vary.
THINK: 10 times; The coin should land heads up half of the time.

Conduct an Experiment 93
   1–5. Experiments will vary.

Is That Fair? 94
   1. Edward
   2. Edward
   3. They have the same number of chances.

Designing a Fair Game 95
   1–2. Games will vary.
DO MORE: Game rules will vary.

Probability 96
   1. pulling a red chip; $\frac{1}{2} > \frac{1}{4}$
   2. rolling an odd number with both number cubes; $\frac{1}{4} > \frac{1}{6}$
   3. peanut butter; There are more peanut butter cookies.
THINK: percents and decimals

Answer Key

The Probability Formula 97
1. $\frac{1}{3}$ 2. $\frac{1}{2}$ 3. $\frac{1}{6}$

THINK: choosing a fourth grader; One-half is greater than the other two fractions.

Probability and Spinners 98
1. $\frac{1}{4}$ 2. $\frac{1}{4}$ 3. $\frac{3}{4}$
4. $\frac{1}{2}$ 5. $\frac{3}{4}$ 6. $\frac{1}{4}$

THINK: 1

Pick a Card 99
1. $\frac{1}{7}$ 2. $\frac{3}{7}$ 3. $\frac{4}{7}$
4. $\frac{3}{7}$ 5. $\frac{4}{7}$ 6. $\frac{1}{7}$

THINK: S

A Decision-Making Spinner 100
1. $\frac{1}{3}$ 2. $\frac{1}{6}$
3. $\frac{1}{2}$ 4. $\frac{2}{3}$
5. 3 to 4

THINK: 5; Bananas are on one-half of the spinner, so Julie should eat bananas half of the 10 days.

Pizza Parlor 101–102

hand-tossed
- pepperoni — hand-toss., pepperoni
- g. peppers — hand-toss., g. peppers
- sausage — hand-toss., sausage
- mushrooms — hand-toss., mushrooms
- onions — hand-toss., onions

thin crust
- pepperoni — thin crust, pepperoni
- g. peppers — thin crust, g. peppers
- sausage — thin crust, sausage
- mushrooms — thin crust, mushrooms
- onions — thin crust, onions

1. 10   2. $\frac{1}{10}$
3. $\frac{1}{10}$ 4. $\frac{1}{2}$
5. $\frac{1}{5}$ 6. 0

THINK: All the outcomes are listed, so you can count the favorable outcomes and possible outcomes.

Getting Dressed 103
1. $\frac{1}{8}$ 2. $\frac{1}{2}$
3. $\frac{1}{4}$

A Probability Riddle 104–105
1. R
2. Y
3. P
4. O
5. B
6. L
PROBABLY

Answer Key

Create Your Own Problems 106
Answers will vary.

Check Your Skills 107–108
1. impossible
2. unlikely
3. certain
4. likely
5. 1, 3, 5
6. 5
7. $\frac{1}{3}$
8.

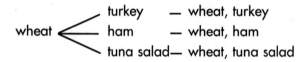

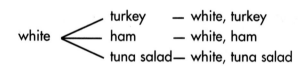

wheat
- turkey — wheat, turkey
- ham — wheat, ham
- tuna salad — wheat, tuna salad

rye
- turkey — rye, turkey
- ham — rye, ham
- tuna salad — rye, tuna salad

white
- turkey — white, turkey
- ham — white, ham
- tuna salad — white, tuna salad

9. 9
10. $\frac{1}{9}$
11. $\frac{1}{3}$

Post Test 109–110
Pictographs will vary. Sample pictograph is shown.

Books Read Last Summer

Jorge	📖 📖 📖 📖 📖 📖
Stewart	📖 📖 📖 📖
Melissa	📖 📖 📖 📖 📖 📖 📖

Key: 📖 = 1 book

1. Melissa
2. 2
3. 4
4. 8
5. $\frac{1}{8}$
6. $\frac{1}{2}$
7. The number of outcomes would double.

bias	bar graph
certain	data
experiment	fact

a way to display data for easier comparison using bars	causes inaccurate results when a sample does not represent the larger group
information	an event that will definitely happen
actual information that can be verified	a method to test a prediction

fair	impossible
likely	line graph
line plot	mean

an event that can never happen	when each person has the same chance of winning
a way to display data that changes over time	an event that has a good chance of happening
the average of a data set	a way to display data along a number line

median	mode
opinion	outcome
outlier	possible

the element of a data set that appears the most	the middle number of a data set when the elements are ordered
possible result of an event	a personal thought or feeling
an event that might happen	a data value that is not typical of the other values in the data set

prediction	probability
range	sample
trend graph	unlikely

number of favorable outcomes / number of possible outcomes	what you think about how likely or unlikely an event is to happen
the people you question that are part of a larger group	the difference between the greatest and the least element of a data set
an event that has a small chance of happening	a bar graph with line segments that show the trend in data over time